salmonpoetry

Diverse Voices from Ireland and the World

MORE PRAISE FOR THIS COLLECTION

'In language both sensual and stark, Felicia McCarthy's poems explore possibilities of re-invention for individuals, species, landscapes. Her work combines the classic American belief in second acts with a woman's intuitive understanding of the pain and courage involved in birth, and in rebirth. McCarthy's voice is flecked with humour, grounded by experience, compelling in its warmth and honesty. Her poems are good company in challenging times.'

Susan Millar DuMars
Author, Ireland & USA

'Drawing on the multiple layered inspirations of history and ancestral memory, the patient strength of the female, and motherhood in its various guises, including Mother Nature herself, this is poetry of elegance and substance. In short, this is a hugely varied and impressive collection.'

Denise O'Hagan
Poet & publisher, Australia

'I can't express enough how powerful this book is. As we see-saw between the personal and historical, between America and Ireland, between patriarchy's stranglehold and matriarchy's promise, I feel a surge of hope that women can inhabit their lives to their fullest potential without retribution of dismissiveness, including their own.'

Sandra Yannone
Poet, USA

the arts council
an chomhairle ealaíon
funding literature

My Country is the Whole World

FELICIA McCARTHY

Published in 2023 by
Salmon Poetry
Cliffs of Moher, County Clare, Ireland
Website: www.salmonpoetry.com
Email: info@salmonpoetry.com

Copyright © Felicia McCarthy, 2023

ISBN 978-1-915022-48-6

All rights reserved. No part of this publication may be reproduced or transmitted in any form or by any means, electronic or mechanical, including photography, recording, or any information storage or retrieval system, without permission in writing from the publisher. The book is sold subject to the condition that it shall not, by way of trade or otherwise, be lent, resold or otherwise circulated without the publisher's prior consent in any form of binding or cover other than that in which it is published and without a similar condition, including this condition, being imposed on the subsequent purchaser.

Cover Image: *'She calls to the Soul Seeds' by Denise Kester*
Cover Design & Typesetting: *Siobhán Hutson Jeanotte*

Printed in Ireland by Sprint Print

Salmon Poetry gratefully acknowledges the support of
The Arts Council / An Chomhairle Ealaíon

For my mother
Margaret McDonough McCarthy
1909-1990
Newspaperwoman, *The Chicago Tribune*
1934-1946

For my own fab four:
Sheelagh, Bren, Kathy, and Clare

and for our fantastic five:
Líní, Julia, Lana, Cate and Seán

Acknowledgements

The author would like to thank the following editors of the many print and online literary zines where some of these poems were first published:

Chris Murray, POETHEAD, an Index of Irish Women Poets
Bernie Crawford et al, SKYLIGHT 47, Ireland
Dave Kavanagh, THE BLUE NIB, Ireland
YSU's editorial team, JENNY, Youngstown State University's literary journal, USA
Carolyn Martin, KRONOS – JOURNAL OF GLOBAL TRANSFORMATION, USA
Jack Little, OFi PRESS, Mexico, and Spain
Shaun Levin, THE A3 REVIEW, UK
Orla Fay and Michael Farry, BOYNE BERRIES, Ireland
Alan Hayes and Nuala O'Connor, eds WASHING WINDOWS III, Arlen House, Ireland.

The author would also like to thank poet and environmental activist and friend, Grace Wells, and the writing duo Susan Millar Dumars and the late Kevin Higgins. These two catalysed a resurgence of creative writing in Galway in the last 20 years with their Over the Edge open mic in Galway City Library and classes at Galway Arts Centre.

Thanks to my writing communities, The Java Writers and The Galway Poets – Bernie Crawford, Anne Irwin, and Marion Cox who took our work on the road and kept going through Covid. A special thanks to my friend, poet Dr Liz Quirke and Fingal County Council's *The Write Time* curator, poet Anne McDonald.

A shout out to award-winning poets Denise O'Hagan and Carolyn Martin for being early readers of this collection. Not to forget TBN's mighty editorial team headed by Dave Kavanagh; Clare Morris, spoken word artist extraordinaire, Emma Lee poet and reviewer of same, and Clara Burghelea, poet and translator at TBN.

Grateful thanks to legend Menna Elfyn, award-winning Welsh poet, for her immediate positive response to my poems and her subsequent endorsement.

My heartfelt thanks to Salmon Poetry and the team of Jessie Lendennie, poet and Siobhán Hutson, design.

Thanks also to Fingal County Council who provided funding for THE SEA, with editor Steve Moore. The anthology raised funds for the RNLI.

The author thanks the Irish Arts Council for the Agility Award which supported the publication of this collection.

Contents

A Note from the Author   11
Foreword by Denise O'Hagan   13

Climate Justice   17
Because You Listen   18
Homage   19
Scriptwriters of a Norse God   20
When I was a Bear in Ireland   21
Bog Magic   22
Pomegranate, A Revision   23
The Ecology of Fire   24
Poet Mother   25
Galway Bay Midsummer   26
If Only We Could Hear the Music of the Spheres   27
Waiting for the Swans   28

Audacious Rendering: The Famine Ship   31
A Photo of My Grandmother the Cyclops   32
Full Circle   33
Mother: A Sequence of Five Poems   34
   The Reader   34
   The Visitor   35
   The Editor   36
   Squaring the Circle   37
   The Companion   37
Kerling   38
Solpadine Dreams   39
Under the Eaves   40
The Ancestors   41

Prediction   45
Waking the Child   46
Train Wreck   47

Power Play	48
After the Storm	49
Mea Maxima Culpa	50
The Price of Fame	51
Triple Zero	52
Medea Explains	53
Mindfulness and Melville	54
People of Extremes	55
I Look for Green and Blue Everywhere	56
Strumpet City	59
Scheherazade in Stephens Green	60
Roll Over JJ – Here Comes Everybody	61
Midwinter Morning	62
The L Word	63
Ode to My T-Shirt	64
Classic Film Noir	65
Marilyn and the Boys	66
The Gypsy Shaman's Daughter	67
Criunniú na mBád	68
Let Morning Come	69
It's the Holidays	73
Hunter Moon Eclipse	74
Everything Waits on the Wind	75
Entrepreneur for My Sex	76
Reading the Omens	77
Fire Dancing at Bealtaine	78
Precession of the Equinoxes	79
The Ferryman is a Woman	80
Finally	81
I am not Waiting	82
Advice from Iowa	83
Notes on Poems	84
Author Bio	86

A Note from the Author

Dear Reader,

Eavan Boland declared she had two countries. Virginia Woolf declared that as a woman, her country was the world. Woolf's remarks were made in Three Guineas, her anti-war protest pamphlet.

I am a woman of two countries, and a woman who belongs to two worlds; the one we live in now that is under reconstruction – a winter transition, perhaps – and the one that is growing within this one, a kinder and more equitable world, I am certain. May we live to see it. May we all do what we can to bring it. May our grandchildren live in it.

You will find love poems to the best of this world, and rants against the worst of it. Be warned that you may not like all that you read. The violent* consequences of a patriarchal world have been suffered by women and children for too long.

I do hope you will be delighted by some of the poems; and angered, amused, awakened by others.

This is my contribution to the changes we are living through. May you find some resonance in your own lives. If you don't, you must write your own. And share them with all of us.

Felicia McCarthy, poet, elder

---

* Third chapter – trigger warning for survivors

Foreword

This debut collection by Felicia McCarthy is well worth the wait: this is poetry of elegance and substance. Drawing on the multiple layered inspirations of history and ancestral memory, the patient strength of the female, and motherhood in its various guises including Mother Nature herself in all her fragile glory, the collection accomplishes that difficult feat of being both delicately composed yet deeply resonant for a contemporary audience. While stopping short of being overtly activist, the poems demand that we be awakened to help realise, in the poet's own words, 'a kinder and more equitable world'.

As its title proclaims, there is a universality to this work, a holistic dimension underpinning it. McCarthy, who has lived in the States as well as Ireland, resists any narrow definition of identity, and in so doing invites us to transcend our own particular background and cultural baggage in favour of one which binds us together. In one of the most memorable poems in the collection, for instance, the poet subtly shifts the spotlight from the punishing journey of a Famine Ship to our own lives in the single deft closing line: 'They've nothing left to lose but all our lives' ('Audacious Rendering: The Famine Ship'). The question, all the more potent for being unasked, hangs in our consciousness: what are we all doing with our lives?

Perhaps the seed of an answer lies in the poet's pervasive sensitivity to the natural world. Time and again, we witness close attention paid to the habits of creatures from giraffes and gnats to gulls and cormorants who, unlike our restlessly acquisitive human race, are 'content to be what they are, / owning naught but their own hollow bones' ('If We Could Hear the Music of the Spheres'). The implication is gentle but unavoidable: we too could choose— or be obliged—to learn to be content with less.

This sort of attention extends to the world of human relationships and domestic interiors, conjured up in succinctly crafted lines such as 'The natural shine of your nose is powder-dusted matte, / your pink cupid bow mouth lip-sticked to red' ('The Visitor'), or in the artful juxtaposition of Othello being quoted to the 'swish of a dishcloth' ('Squaring the Circle'). Equally adept on the wider political stage, the poet is unsparing in her condemnation of corruption in high places, as in 'There is silence in the Vatican …/ There is silence from the small god of men' ('Mea Maxima Culpa') or the poem beginning with the memorable line, 'Picasso's women never had a chance / to be real') ('The Price of Fame').

In a collection studded with so many splendid poems, those inspired by ancient mythology deserve special mention and will surely take their place among the already distinguished poems in this vein. 'Pomegranate, A Revision', a retelling of the Greek myth of Persephone, seduces from the very start: 'Nine seeds were all it took / to thicken the plot into a myth…'; 'Medea Explains', another daring interpretation of an ancient myth with the piercing wrap-up line, 'I loved you too much to let you die by inches'; 'The Gypsy Shaman's Daughter', evoking the ancient visionary wisdom and power of the woman with lines such as 'In the final hour, women / sing strength and rise'; and 'The Ferryman is a Woman', recasting Charon, ferryman of the dead to Hades, as an old woman with a wicked tongue: 'Sure it isn't / the end of the world, she says with a grin'.

This is an accomplished entrée to the contemporary poetry scene by a highly gifted writer. Yet as poet Martyn Crucefix puts it, 'Poetry can never be summarised by its own conclusions', and it is in the reading of poems and the response that they wreak in each of us that they come fully alive. I urge you to pick up this collection and give it the time it so richly deserves.

DENISE O'HAGAN
award-winning poet and editor of Black Quill Press. Sydney, Australia

(Source for quote from *Crucefix: Influences on 'Between a Drowning Man' #2* | Martyn Crucefix)

*'There is no freedom without fear and bravery there is no
freedom unless
earth and air and water continue and children
also continue
It is the responsibility of the poet to be a woman to keep an eye on
this world and cry out like Cassandra but be
listened to this time'*

– from *Responsibility* by GRACE PALEY
poet, writer, teacher, and political activist, 1922-2007

Climate Justice

October brings all
that July held back.

Sun in a clear sky,
dry, for more than a day.
Fog, both early and late.

In the blue dark morning
the red light of Venus
signals a warning.

At dusk a mist rises
to hide the setting sun
from the change and loss

we must now weather
together.

Because You Listen

after Adrienne Rich

In such times as these it is no longer
necessary to talk about trees, which way
grass grows, how roads sheer to shadow,
abandoned meeting houses, or the disappeared.

But here, not somewhere else, as the world
arrives at the darkest of its fears, the dread
is constant, as the invisible has its way
sweeping through the population.

Because you listen to the poets, we come
together to talk about science, words, and remedies
and women's work of watching, keeping things
going. We have some experience with patience.

The wolf boys cry out and hoard supplies.
The elders, particularly the grandmothers,
gather curing weeds and heirloom seeds,
and prepare to call everyone to the table.

Homage

The giraffes
purr among themselves
at a frequency none of us hear.

Does it matter?
Their affairs are their own.
And what they have to say about us
is irrelevant to anything happening in
the world we believe is the only one.

Or so they say.
We place ourselves above all
the planet's breathing life forms, we
know little or nothing. Mountains breathe,
did you know? They whistle on the outbreath.
You may think it is the air shuffling about
their peaks. No. Generations of humans
live and die, love and leave to return
again, before the end of one
momentous exhalation.

Sweet living Christ,
Show some
respect.

Scriptwriters of a Norse God

At dawn, a cloud of finger-wingéd crows
flies into the forecourt at The Osprey.
Like a bee swarm, it sails between walls,
waking us with joyous, raucous calls.

This is Odin's tribe, these his messengers
their feathers the ink, the air the page,
their song the prelude. Their script is a fleeting
sketch of sacred geometry, a dizzying

Escher print, animated and vocal.
*Life, Death! It is all the same. We are
all carrion or soon will be.* It's time for us
to wake and unscramble the design drawn

by a murder of crows. It's time to listen
to this gypsy cabal of birds, who prophesy
the ending, without using words.

When I was a Bear in Ireland

my home place was Knockma
where moss grows a thick cushion over stones,
knits green ganseys for the trunks and arms of
beech and ash, trees that reach for heaven.

Tall guardians of the sacred cairns,
keepers of the magic of folk, stand with me
as I listen to the long soft rain *ping and ping*
to wet the brown leaves of autumn.

The sound brings the memory of Lough Corrib
and feasting on its red-fleshed salmon, the lush
hedgerows of blackberry and sloe, and honey
from the hives hidden the sycamore.

In the cave below the grave of Finvarra, King of Faery
and Maeve, Queen of Connaught, my brown cubs
grew fat on the milk I made from the rich lap of Éire.
When I was a bear in Ireland, my home place was Knockma.

Bog Magic

We walked lightly onto land
that is half water, part bone and blood
mud root and branch, us and not us.
The sun slipped behind a cloud.
I could see the mist at the foot of
The Twelve Pins held the ghosts
of those who had drawn too close,
and were held fast by ancient gods
demanding fresh thoughts.

I let fall the sharp-stemmed bog flowers,
clutched the silk wrap against a sudden chill
as our feet walked over another part of me
ripening below from sinew to bark and stone
deep within the dark breathing earth
where life goes on beginning again
with water, clay, and fire.

Pomegranate, A Revision

Nine seeds were all it took
to thicken the plot into a myth
that cut the year in half,
and half again.

Sticky when wet, the pink
and gold skin of the fruit is thin
but tough. A sharp blade, a swift
slap on the black granite

countertop creates a path for the red
juice to drip along your fingers, wetting
your wrists. The bright seeds glisten
in the air as if aching to be spooned.

Nine seeds consumed in the dark
was enough cause a cleft in the earth
with time left for the daughter to find
her lover in the underworld.

Ceres settles by the hearth to rest,
trusts her daughter and years of
good mothering. Persephone returns
a woman, pregnant with Spring.

The Ecology of Fire

May 25, 2018*

After the Yellowstone fire
everything changed. What was old
died, and what was dead, burned.

Seeds that had waited buried deep
in the forest floor for one hundred
years or more, for lightening to strike

and set the trees alight, were ready.
The trees' green canopies played
toss with fire across streams

and the fresh dug firebreaks.
They lobbied the fireball for miles,
as if this were a game of hot potato.

Old Faithful belched sulphur.
Helicopters dumped lakes.
The forests burned on.

People died fighting to save themselves
or something else. The trees, like mothers
who know the future depends on them, tossed on.

And the seeds
born of fire
split open.

Poet Mother

for Liz

Don't let the baby swallow your words,
the ones that arrive in the night
as you swaddle her, singing.
Repeat into her tiny ears the rhymes
you will write in the morning.

She won't mind what it is, as long
as you sing softly and rock her gently
in the rhythm of your next poem.
This will keep the words from
stifling you, from choking her.

She loves all your creations.
The lines you remember at dawn
will become the maps she will take
away from these sweet days
and nights in your arms.

Galway Bay Midsummer

after Tu Fu

Black gnats dance
along the inner pane of my open window.
The water below
is calm and grey in the darkening evening

The tidal stream appears
on the bay's still surface to be a foam snake
meandering toward the Cliffs of Moher
as the lights of Ballyvaughn beckon.

And I would have wagered my heart
was already full when suddenly the moon
rose above Claddagh, looking for all the
world, like the apricots I ate for breakfast.

If We Could Hear the Music of the Spheres

They skywrite their ease ignoring boundaries,
a mixed flock of birds heralds the great storm.

Crows and gulls fall and rise together
sailing in time to the one celestial score.

A cormorant opens her wings as if to bless
the fleet of swans sailing by on the tide.

All of these are content to be what they are,
owning naught but their own hollow bones,

feet, feather, beak, and wing –
all of the earth, the whole of the sky.

Waiting for the Swans

I walk from Salthill along the causeway
to the Corrib and pause at a bench. My stillness
is so complete, a gull swoops close, then veers
off to circle above the fast waters of the tide.
I wait for the swans to land.

At sunrise they arrive, two at a time,
wide bodies thinned by reaching necks,
the long stretch to the shallows in sight.
White dashes of morse code signal morning.
Slowly they drop wings like flags of surrender

as they let go the wide sky for the quick
changing current of the river.
Anchored light. I rise grateful, plant
my boots on the scree of Claddagh quay
and turn for home.

*'We think back through our mothers
if we are women.'*

– Virginia Woolf
A Room of One's Own

Audacious Rendering: The Famine Ship

for sculptor, John Behan and my ancestors

From the forge of his imagination came a boat
out of the past, carrying an empire's shame and our ancestors.
Audacious rendering. The sight of it knocked the wind from my sails.
Moorings loose, my mind slips as the body remembers.

Hands grip the masts of a ship too small to hold them all,
and they ride the wind as if born to it. Open mouths
catch the sea spray to clean the brown slime of blight
from their throats, seaweed stains from their teeth.

Thin as the sheets of sailcloth they replace, their flesh
sways in the breeze, rags on a line whipped by the wind.
Larger than life they are, on an ocean without an edge.
Despair or hope must hold them fast.

They've nothing left to lose but all our lives.

A Photo of My Grandmother the Cyclops

for Maggie McDonough

squints behind thick glasses, tilts her head
and looks sharp into the camera. Across the
lines of time, the white-haired granny nails me.

Maggie the Cyclops furnished the house
with her pinochle winnings. She loved cards
with her friends and jokes with her sons.

The eldest made her laugh, all but one died young.
My grandmother the Cyclops fanned the Treasures
of a Poetic World with chapped fingers, scarred thumbs.

The book sat like a bible on the kitchen counter,
near to hand when time from housework allowed.
I imagine the white pages whip the air, cooling

her lovely worn face. I hear the thwap! as she finds
her place and begins to murmur aloud the lines. For
our Cyclops, the sound of poetry was a Siren song.

The mule that took her right eye is long dead.
The cataract that clouded the left came with age.
The lines she learned by heart stayed to the end of days.

Full Circle

I am from corn, hot Iowa miles of it, and the smell of ether
seeping from a leather bag on top of the fridge. I am from
pony men and card sharks, drunks, and steam engine train drivers.
I am from blue pencil marks on galley proofs, typed on an upright
Royal. I am from screen doors slapping against armies of Canadian
soldiers. I am from the dog days of August, the ice storms
of winter, and the frozen mud-trenched roads of spring.

I am from a lake that died and a river that burned, from the Erie
the Cuyahoga, and a town called Ashtabula. I am from ore boats
on the horizon with the foghorn sounding a warning across the lake
on a still autumn night. I am from the Bascule bridge, the brick yards,
the rail yards, and a back yard that held a Great Lake. I am from
a ham-fisted man with a fedora and a black skirted priest; both
with whiskey breath and an enviable reach.

I am from among her effects: The loose powder box of pasteboard
stuffed with old letters. *My dearest Girl*, I read, and *Dear Grand Girl*.

I am from tenant farmers on Mayo's *Foot of the Reek*
to McCarthy's farm on Allegheny's Black Creek, finally
returned from the forced migration known as an Gorta Mór. *

---

* The Great Hunger

Mother: A Sequence of Five Poems

after May Sarton

I. THE READER

Once more
I summon you out of the past
with my querulous love.

Today I remember
the adventuring mother
my own Marco Polo
whose China was the library
whose exotic spices were books.

You travelled once a week
to the Carnegie in the harbour
returned with stacks to sort through
dip into, you'd say, since each book
was tested before you dove in.

At dawn, I would find you
in the honey maple chair,
pushed back from the
kitchen table with its yellow
lino top. I can smell

the burnt toast, see the black
crumbs on the cobalt blue plate,
the butter grease slick
on the gone cold coffee.
I hear your soft chuckle

in the hall where I hide.
I watch your ring flash
as you turn the page,
stealing one more moment
before the work begins.

II. THE VISITOR

I see you upright in the visitor's chair
set back from the bed. You are not my mother

but the doctor's wife with church hat and veil,
your best coat unbuttoned but kept on, white cotton

gloves in the hand that holds the patent leather purse
close-to on your soft bellied lap. You are a working

man's daughter, dressed up to meet your husband's
place in his world. It is known the nurses take note.

Immobilized by a brace, I watch puzzled as you
you become a stranger, out of our usual context,

yet the same woman who brings forbidden treats-
Clark bars, Betty and Veronica comics.

Isolated by glass, the smell of Clorox and floor wax,
I wait for the familiar touch of your clean dry hand.

The natural shine of your nose is powder-dusted matte,
your pink cupid bow mouth lip-sticked to red.

We are in your husband's church, this one you leave
too soon, after you tattoo my forehead with your lips,
to show you'd been in the room.

III. THE EDITOR

In those days *good fences made for good neighbours*.
A wave from the yard sufficed for friendliness.
You kept your distance, your separateness intact
even, especially, from us.

And what I remember after your constant reading
is the sound of your fingers striking typewriter keys
of the upright Royal in the clickety-clack
talk of the *small little things*. You edited out

the hard times, let the violence be muffled by distance
and the heavy oak door of the old stone house,
set behind the big tree studded yard, enclosed
by the red bricked fence. After writing

you might turn on the gas under the dented
tarnished copper kettle, invite me to find
the freeze-dried coffee, our favourite mugs
and sit with you on the concrete porch.

Together we read our separate stories
and sipped the bittersweet brew in silence
while you waved to all passers-by,
the neighbours, the strangers.

IV. Squaring the Circle

Last, I remember you saved your best attention
for Shakespeare, and the nonsense poetry of Edward Lear.
The heroines of Willa Cather were yours, pioneers
of the western high plains, making much from little,
managing to survive and even, to sing.

I am left with the sound of your voice quoting *Othello*,
the swish of the dishcloth as you wipe the black
and white countertop, and the sweet steam of cinnamon
sugar escaping from your deep-dish apple pie
as it cools on a rack by the door.

V. The Companion

Here in the future, I return
to the sheltering arms of the library
where you wait for me, reading quietly.
Sometimes, I think I hear you humming
an old song until you remember the words.

Kerling*

for Sheila

Your blouses are stained.
The belly of your trousers catches the drip.
Food drops from your fork more often than not,
on its way to your mouth. Your eyes clouded by age,
your fingers reshaped to another form. Your hands
nowadays remind me of a bird's feet clutching
an empty branch in late winter, holding on in spite
of the weather and the absence of peers.

One by one, unconsciously it seems
you shut down your physical systems,
the way you used to close down the house
late on a winter night. I remember how
you made your own way through the dark.
You say you dream of going home. Yet you
move so slowly toward that door, I wonder.
As a child, I was certain you were brave.

I used to listen from my bed as you
pulled in and locked tight each window
against the Lake chill. I'd hear the curtain rings
slide along their tracks as you darkened the room.
A quiet then as you turned down the heat.
The snap of every light switch told me
where you were in your nightly routine.

The old floorboards creaked in places all of us
knew, charting your journey toward the stair.
The third and fourth step telegraphed your ascent
until I heard your muffled tread on the oval rug
in the hall. One by one, you tucked us in,
calmed our fears with a soft chiding whisper
as you walked away into the dark.

* Old woman

Solpadine Dreams

Unexpectedly she rose from the dead.
Returned she said, to save me from myself
and my skewed view of her. Apples baking
with cinnamon sugar, her famous pie
gave warning she was on her way.

She rose, in her apron, at the end of the bed
and said, *pick that up and follow me!*
So, I did and we were off

out of the window, into the grey slick
of an early April morning, in the non-light
to sit in her boat at the centre of the Lake.
Look up, she said.

The sun was roaring down toward the horizon.
The moon was a white ball in the sky, batted
between the twin stars of the Gemini. I watched
as if it were the Wimbledon final and this dream
was real.

The moon rocketed back and forth across the star
diamond net of the Milky Way as she spoke,
I gave you the whole world and poetry.

Under the Eaves

The first away is a brown-eyed beauty.
Chestnut hair, released from its band
fans to cover the white pillow. Sweat
moistens the upper lip, curls the wisps
of hair as she slides down into sleep.
Her seven-year-old body folds proteins
into neat stacks after another day's
frustration. She dreams tomorrow
will make more sense.

In the room below is the golden-haired girl.
Her blue eyes move quickly under closed lids
as she scans this newest day of her six years.
She turns constantly and kicks off the duvet.
Her clogged bronchi are heard in the hallway
sounding like the rasp and rev of uilleann pipes.
She dreams of breathing easy the cool air
at the top of the Sugar Loaf.

Nearby is the last at four and a half,
already beyond all our reckonings.
Her hazel eyes spark with defiant mirth.
She cannot rest with the stories jump-starting
in her head, the songs tumbling from her mouth.
Suddenly she sleeps, her engine in neutral.
She dreams of riding out into the world
on the back of her mother's dark horse.

The Ancestors

are always with us
like gravel on Baille strand*
like sand in shoes, always near,
shuffling socked feet, looking for attention.

Sharp noses poke through the curtain of time.
Pride and scorn drip from pointing fingers.
We were side-lined too soon, I watch them
shout, their mouths moving in mime.

Their empty bodies are flat and bagged
like clothes back from the dry cleaners –
their skin empty of flesh, inside out pockets
flapping loose in an ethereal breeze.

At the edge of time our ghosts beg
for one more day among us here in the light.
They show up in the chins and the eyes of our children.
There is no end to their desire to return, make things right.

* Mary Heaney, *Nine Waves*

'I write to comfort the afflicted and to afflict the comfortable.'

– Lucille Clifton
African American poet, 1936-2010

Prediction

Years ago, you said,
Saved for a worse fate!
a midwestern cliché
spoken with such relish,
its meaning blew past
my small ears.

Years gone by, I see
the fate you saved me from
is long forgotten
while the fate you saved me for
arrived today
with the heavy freight
of all you promised.

Waking the Child

You took a great piece of my life
and are stealing it still.
Long buried, like Christ
you rise on the third day,
to stall my momentum.

Each time you come, I am
lifted again from a stunned body.
Teeth clenched, breath caught,
I keep still, as instructed,
and wait for the devil to be done.

My neck is bowed with the shame,
my small back bowed further again.
Still, I carve memory into words,
load it into this frame.

Train Wreck

Like a building without cladding,
or a person without skin, you are
more vulnerable than the rest.
You were not made for this world
with its criss-cross currents
of sight and sound and smell,
and yet here you are
cutting parts of your body
to ease the strain and force a fit.
Yours is the bloodied Procrustean bed.

The train of events performs
the bat trick of echolocation
and each sensory nerve
of your being
screams

Hide!
Here comes the 9:45.

Power Play

I thought you had finally gone
from my life when suddenly you
you waft back into the room
on the acrid scent seeping from
a tin of black shoe polish.

We are engaged again in that old dance.
My back to you, my hands gone numb
in the cold grey dishwater and I freeze
in place, as always when you say,
Be Still.

After the Storm

for Knute Skinner whose poem 'Let's Just Say' inspired the last line

Imagine the winter dark and the fire lit,
pine resin hisses on the iron grate and the stench
of the burning sap fills the many-windowed room.

The green kindling is slow to catch
until the flame penetrates its small crevices.
Then the sweet wood burns blue and gold

like a diamond match. A loud report as the wood
splits throwing live sparks into your lap.
There is no fire screen.

A gale force torments the windows
and they rattle in response inside their casements.
Outside, squalls strip branches from trees,

slap limbs against the cold stone house.
Twigs strum the panes like a child's nails
tapping at the glass, small sounds

easily missed, but we hear and look up and out
into the dark yard, faces pressed to the cold glass,
hands like visors around our eyes wondering who is there.

The hail swarms down from the black
tower of cloud to torture the red tiled roof
as loud and fast as a gatling gun.

Let's just say you will never feel safe again.

Mea Maxima Culpa*

'They buried me. They didn't know I was a seed.'
—Sinéad O'Connor

J'accuse! the deaf man shouted.
Father Murphy shrugged and called for
Silence! from this lamb of God
who suffered in the House of God
in the private sacristy.

There is silence in the Vatican
among the appointed bishops of men.
Clad in black dresses sashed with red
they take tea and cake in the afternoon
as they vie for the power of infallibility.

There is silence from one small god of men
as he removes the red shoes of the Fisherman.
Two popes now live in the Vatican, both deaf
and silent to testimony. Paedophile priests roam
free to feast like wolves on the lambs of God,
the innocent children of the blind faithful.

The Price of Fame

Picasso Museum, Malaga, 2017

Picasso's women never had a chance
to be real, even now.
They chose to let go of being themselves
for the glamour of being chosen.
Two will go mad, two will use their own
hands to kill themselves.

If you look close you find contortion
in place of the faces he claimed to love.
Each portrait is a skin stretched to a board,
coloured by the master's need to control. In this
21st century world, women begin to realise
their throats can do more than swallow.

The fractures on their faces are his.
The extra eye and head, his duplicity.
A single giant breast, with one sharp
titillating nipple reveal the heart of his story.

Picasso martyred women
not for art, but to nail his fear onto canvass.
Buyers agree.
Women are difficult, naturally.
Best to reduce them to fractions.

And frame them.

Triple Zero

after reading a BBC report on the change in Western women's clothes sizes

She's worn thin
like the soles of her shoes,
like the shine on a dime.

She holds herself tall,
and quiet as if she were a stick
and might snap.

She takes her place in space
a faceless lacquered mannikin
and hardly moves at all.

Except in the morning,
when she leaves in the dark,
the cold almost-but-not-quite dawn.

She pulls on her triple-zero gear,
ties her all-terrain shoes into knots,
carefully stretches her quads

and runs for her life.

Medea Explains

*for Toni Morrison and Margaret Garner**

I saved them, my lad and lassie,
Memory and Fleuris, little beloveds
saved them from rape or worse.
When Jason turned away from us,
his wife and children and toward Glauce
the new, younger me? I knew without
his protection we were left vulnerable.
I am your mother. I had to protect you.

It was not easy to win the battle between
a mother's instinct to protect her children
over my real experience of the world's cruelty.
But I did it, my little ones, sharp and quick.
I had to save you from the torture that was certain.
I loved you too much to let you die by inches.

Mindfulness and Melville

All this talk of mindfulness
is as useless as dead air on the radio.
Minds weren't meant to be still

minds were made to be used; come with lifetime guarantees –
mostly. Don't empty your mind. Download gigabytes of data.
You can create fresh paths in those neural networks.

Repeat the old mantra, *Tune in, turn on*
but please, don't *drop out* or down into the lotus position.
And kindly refrain from repeating a sonorous *Om*.

The men wanting to sell me a still mind
are the same as politicians and priests, glad to mansplain,
bully and shame women to sit down and stay quiet.

All this talk of being here now from so many great white males,
ignites a spark in our rebel women's hearts, conjures a vision of
a triple masted schooner equipped with sharp, well-oiled harpoons.

People of Extremes

for working class Dems whose anger is manipulated by a wannabe king

I come from people who break the rules
because they have money. Some of my people
break the rules because they have none.

I come from people who lost their hearts
in the rat race. Some of my people are mean,
some cruel. They don't enjoy living

as much as running lives not their own. Some
of my people have ideas and won't be crossed
by the people they deem beneath them.

All were fighters, rebels, survivors. Some of my people
drank themselves to to an early death, or lived too long
with people who wished they had.

Righteous or wrong-headed, none of my people ever give up.
When they go down, they won't be going alone.

I Look for Green and Blue Everywhere

I find women like me any place
beauty might strike us dumb.

Awed, by a shot of light
streaking from an break in the cloud,

or the floodlit moon as it makes a path
to treasures at the end of dark waters.

Like me, they never let a good thing pass.
We are seekers of pleasure with good

reason. We know the sudden grasp
of talons into our feathered backs,

the abrupt end of childish thoughts
as a clumsy bill gnaws the soft neck.

The mind drifts away, as it must,
to find something that is beautiful,

some heavenly thing to hold us, and hold onto-
something that will keep us tethered to this earth.

'The hand was the fire and the page tinder'

– Eavan Boland
Irish poet, 1944-2020
from 'The Lost Art of Letter Writing'

Strumpet City

On this early Spring morning,
the bay looks a grubby lace petticoat
dragging below a grey skirt of sky.

Dirty old Dublin wakes and strips
herself of yesterday's chances.
With a moist wind she clears

the gritty remains of the night
beneath the black pools of her eyes.
No one cares until she conjures up a cold shower,

puts on her best rose lavender dress,
sets the gold torque at her throat, the silver
crescent moon into the clouds of her hair.

And we are once more, beguiled.

Scheherazade in Stephen's Green

It never should have happened that way
on that day in that park where once
they lay in the high grass, lost in
in the love between them.

Now it was late in the year, late
on a Sunday, near closing time.
They walked apart passed the empty
playground, the meadow of blown flowers.

No one about. No one heard her
keen nor saw his façade crumble.
Her anger, his sorrow, grief doubled.
The loss of the dream, a single lament.

Penelope, weaver of hope; Scheherazade,
postponing the inevitable with tall tales.
Truth brought a torch to burn the book,
thread and frame to the ground.

They parted at Fusilier's Arch, the exit
Dubliners christened Traitor's Gate.

Roll Over JJ – Here Comes Everybody

for Molly and Bloom, JJ and Nora and all lovers of Ben Eader

Golden furze blaze from Muck Rock,
my perch at the top of Ben Eader, while
ferns the size of small cottages leap to hide
Aideen's cromlech from strangers.

It is Bealteane and Eadin's hill is a skyscraper
of colour. Bursts of white rhododendron flaunt
hearts of black cherry, orange stamens
signal readiness with fragrance and pollen.

Red, pink, and purple flowers fall to mix
with dry pine needles. Centuries of Springs
make a deep bed of black peat that pushes
back against my booted footsteps.

I watch the tides of Dublin Bay and North Shore
sweep in to lick and kiss the neck of Sutton. Howth
castle walls will turn to sand, the flowers flourish and fall
as lovers return to make love on the soft scented hill of Eadin.

Midwinter Morning

First light comes late
this midwinter morning.
Too soon we wake from
our cave of dreams
to a room lit only

by the constellations.
Too long must we wait
for the sun to chase away the stars
and shake the sparkling dust
from the black blanket of night.

Let us be careless of such glories,
as we fall laughing
into the warm embrace
of what beauty lies here
in our own fleshy story.

Let the world this once
bring the lantern of light
to open the doors of day
without word or witness
from either of us.

The L Word

Love is a thing of twoness.
— D.H. Lawrence

The rock and the roll of it
the neck-arcing ache of it
the soft honeyed silence
at the beginning and end of it
the sweet tender risk of it
the quiet quickening of it
the sound of your heart
beating in sync with mine.

The dear sweat and wet of it
the swelling tide smell of it
the heat at the height of it
the depth and the breadth
of the give and the take
we sleep and vow to keep
passion and love alive, beshert.
We have both *world enough, and time.**

---

* Andrew Marvel, to his coy mistress.

Ode to My T-Shirt

for Nora, BFF

You were my secret agent, perfect blue T
from the swinging Sixties, dropcloth to
the heavy fall of hair the colour of honey.

In Walden, your moody blue became an
anchor in the green sea of grass, an arrow
in the white birch wood near the grave.

Boat neckline shored up below the long pier
of my throat, falling just so, to drape gently
against those young vulnerable hips.

Perfect T, fabric ripped free from a slamming
screen door of an Ohio farmhouse, it was you
who held the decade of my well spent youth.

I was a rebel with many a cause and you the flag
declaring my absolute belief in beauty and truth.
Time softened the fabric to lavender, the colour
often found at the beginning and ending of days.

Classic Film Noir

after Edna St Vincent Millay

My nemesis has no clothes, she does not live in the light
but ah, my friends, and oh, my foes, bring on the bracing night.

Soon we will move together, to a different time and space,
live without these bodies, our sweet instruments of grace.

Who'd be without such glory? No shock, we've struck a deal
to stay on earth caught up upon its spinning karmic reel.

Without the light, no dark, no darkness without the light.
Now! We'll take another turn, in flickering black and white.

Marilyn and the Boys
for JFK

I didn't die that time, Mr President.
I left the building with Elvis.
At 2am he drove up in that
pink fin-tail Cadillac of his
just as I was about to sink
into the valley of the dolls.
MAR-lin, he said, calling my name
in that Memphis boy drawl of his,
Y'all can't let 'em win the game.

We left for Vegas lickety-split, drove 'cross
the sands to the land of plenty good 'nough.
He wears my best sequins and I wear his,
we make a living as look a-likes. You know,
that last life was fine with you, Bob, and Jimmy
but this is better where all I gotta do is throw
the dice to decide who I wanna be that day.
The pay's steady, and we're jess like 'em,
Yer real good, they say.

The Gypsy Shaman's Daughter *

The Burren air trembles at the sound of stone
castanets thrummed by a red-shirted goddess
ready to emerge onto land. The staccato bursts
leap from Liscannor to The Twelve Pins and back.

The gypsy shaman stands, implants the Cliffs
of Moher for teeth and heaves her great bulk forward.
A limestone mantle covers the hills of her shoulders,
soft heather lines her chest, golden gorse cinches her waist.

Her great breasts, plumped by pregnancy and millennial drift,
point toward the land we call The End of the World.
She sets one foot over The Arans, while the other
covers all the bog from Spidéal to Oughterard.

Tectonic plates shift as our gypsy goddess wades
into Galway Bay. She reaches back to the Burren
steal the dolmen stones of Poulnabrone.
As Odin cast the future with runes, our queen

rolls the querns like dice in the skin drum of her fist
before tossing them into the Atlantic. The waves
stream up in liquid mountains whose tops curl
in quick-spinning green spirals. The earth quakes

five days and six nights. The sea dissolves all the land
in sight. Darkness falls and keeps falling until black
reigns and all are blind. In the final hour, women
sing strength and rise. A new world is born
from the heart of the gypsy shaman's thighs.

Cruinniú na mBád – The Gathering of the Boats

Trussed up in their Sunday best, blood red
and black sails billowing, the Hookers fly
across the Bay, rounding the buoy set out
for the race. There is a place for everything.

Full sails burst into view as I crest the hill
of Dalysfort Road where I played a game
Dodge-ems with the *Bóthar na Trá* from
town. There is a place for everything.

I had left my heart in Shannon with daughters
taking planes going elsewhere. Of a sudden, it
thumped back and I laughed out loud to see these
racy old girls competing in their Galway colours.

There is a place for everyone.
And I was back in mine.

Fishing Off the Pyramids

Ashtabula, Ohio

we were a couple
trying new angles
till the children came

our interest stretched
in order to form
a more perfect union

we added a base
its points placed
in the four directions

we had depth, breadth, height
on a square foundation
like the kids we were

we took turns on top
to think like a trout
and fish for walleye

along the break wall
of The Great Lakes
golden brown tinged

blocks of armour stone
whipped sideways and
piled high like pyramids

by the force of the waves
repeating themselves
over and over

Let Morning Come

after Jane Kenyon

Let the street lamps blink out,
the lights of Ballyvaughn grow dim,
as darkness gives way to day.

Let the shush-shush of the tides
slide into your dream, beckon you awake,
to open your eyes. Let morning come.

Let the sky lift her grey skirts,
draw up her shawl of cloud, the
way the curtain must rise before the play.

To the heron strutting along the shore,
to gulls drifting above the bay, to lovers
making love in their beds, let morning come.

Let the gold disc deliver on its promise.
Let the wind come up. Let the fishing boats
sail from safe harbours. Let morning come.

Let it come, as it will, and don't keep
yourself back. The world begins
fresh each day, so let morning come.

'As a woman I have no country.

As a woman I want no country.

As a woman my country is the whole world.'

– *from* Three Guineas
VIRGINIA WOOLF, 1882-1941

It's the Holidays

and I am popping red
corns from a pomegranate
into the morning yoghurt.

Winter rattles the window
an easterly buffets the door,
a trespass to draw the heat

into the maw and teeth
of a Siberian wind.
As determined in effort

as I, in my quest to draw
comfort from the bright
red kernels tucked into

a papery thin catacomb
of bitter pith. Just like
Christmas with its

flimsy tissue paper
wrapped tight round
the prize waiting inside.

It is New Year's Eve
and this is enough; a thin
juice as sweet as needed

to cure the sour from a year.
I lick my wrist fingers and lips
with a pleasure born of lack.

Hunter Moon Eclipse

Last night, a red clad moon called
me awake from a dream of Mars—
of fire, flames, and hidden reservoirs.

She called me down to the abandoned
streets, out to the clean sweep of strand.
Even the wind was elsewhere.

Like a voyeur, I watched the slow
uncovering of light and dark, the formal
mating dance of the moon and her lover.

This morning the moon rose
naked, but for a nimbus of gold
and never called to me at all.

Everything Waits on the Wind

to deliver winter wildness.
Gulls especially, want the high
of falling onto a fast-tracking stream.
Like a panting breath, the waves beat
until broken open into foam, roll
until slammed into the sand.
It's a circus.

Everyone waits on the wind
to deliver winter's sleep
like the boy with arms raised
Up! up! to his best beloved dad,
trees stretch up to touch the wind,
feel its fingers rumple their crowns,
brush away the year's harvest of leaves
and put them gently to bed.

Entrepreneur for My Sex

for Emily, Kim, Vona, Nuala, Adrienne et al.*

This is no time for regret, or the wet
wool drag of it on your shoulders,
the stale sour smell of waste. I am
wanton and wide awake. What feelings
are these, what is this bright, vital buzz.
Blood sizzles through muscle lighting
signal fires across the nerve plexus.

Eyes wide I stride, sashay these hips
so glad. Ba-Boom, blood beats in the heart,
its muscle holds the life-giving liquid
for a split second, only to send it out again
plumped up with oxygen until the body fires
up and I am panting, breathless with the heat.
The body wants this drumbeating exaltation.

It loves the lavish fireworks, the pop and fizz
of sight sound and smell, the beat and repeat
of yes. The body will sing its spirit song.

Come closer. Which of you fears the fire?
Who among you has a taste for flame?
No matter, I'm a self-starter.

Reading the Omens

A chorus of voices called, *No!*
when I reached for the latch.
Don't let her out, she'll die.

A monarch hatched from the rafters.
Her orange and black wings a mirror
of the hot coals that had waked her.

A trail of twisted cobweb sported flies
as if it were a kite tail tied with bows
and she ready to be launched into the sky.

Though we turned away
she is with me still, as I
plan for the days ahead.

Take this as written:
when my time comes
to launch from this body

I want you to open the window.

Fire Dancing at Bealtaine

We make seats of the rocks at Spidéal beach after a walk on the
cooling strand. She says, *look at the waves through squinted eyes.*

The sunlight falling on the water looks like little fires dancing
upward toward the faint shell of the moon. It might be a requiem

for winter, a bonfire honouring Baal, or the world welcoming
you into its wider arms as you leave the safety of mine.

We watched a thousand lights lick the hollows of the waves
till the water of the harbour goes up in flames. At our back

the flowers of the horse chestnut flicker like lit candles. This
picture is a faint mirror of the splendour ahead as you follow a
path across these waters, taking you far away from Spidéal pier.

Precession of the Equinoxes

There was always going to be a reckoning.
Inhale, exhale, examine the ebb and flow of tide.
Watch the moon's effect on the water, on your
changing energy, thoughts, your pride.

The fall and rise were written in at the start.
We make theatre, poetry, and art from the pain
of misunderstanding the bigger picture. Consider
the outer planets, solar winds, the moon's white shadow.

Each full spin of the axis lasts thousands of years.
Each turn upward on the spiral brings another reckoning
of truth, half-truths, and the inevitable uncovering of lies.

The Ferryman is a Woman
for Chariklo

The old lad who hides his face in his hood
with the shadow of a scythe on his shoulder
has put his wife on the job while he takes a time out
on Mars, or Venus, somewhere out in the stars.

The wife is as cushioned as Charon was edgy,
stooped as he was tall, but soft with it all.
Like the rest of us, she needs the work, can use
a bit of pin money, the gold coin of passage
left in the mouth, the coppers covering the eyes.

She shows her face, no hoodies here,
just a white net over her flying-away hair.
When I arrive at death's door, she invites me in
to sit while she puts on the kettle. *Sure it isn't
the end of the world*, she says with a grin.

But it is, and this cat is on her ninth life,
ready to move on to the next thing.
Are you sure now, think about it. So, I do.

I remember the water and the trees,
fields of wild strawberry, milk thistle
and dandelion seeds drifting on the breeze.
Raven, gulls, *I will miss them all indeed
but I've more to do beyond the body,
and I am travelling light, you see.*

Finally

it all comes together
what you have done and left undone.

The rain roars
in from the northeast.
Wind steals the breath right from your mouth.

Above, gulls
play tag with dark crows
darting in and out of thermal layers.

In between
these two worlds you must
choose to struggle or be at home

where nothing
matters now but this
low winter sunlight and high wind

flying clean
through you as if you'd
finally forgiven those who left you

here, where the
rolling waves scoop stone
bone and shell into a polished finish.

I Am Not Waiting*

for a good man to show up
    for my life to begin
    for the world to wake up
        to equality and climate justice

not waiting
    for my ship to come in
    or the boat to go out
    to collect the refugees forced
        from the birthplace of our race

not waiting, no
    for the approval of peers
    or the clearance of the last trace of survivor's guilt

I am not waiting
    for the second coming, nor even, come to think of it, the first

not waiting
    for the children to grow, to settle
    for bills to be paid
    for violence against women to end
        and poverty to be a thing of the past.

We do not have that kind of time.
We cannot wait
for Ferlinghetti's rebirth of wonder, instead
    we must birth our own

We are women in a chaotic age
    who gather and share
    what is found there:
        water, food, and shelter
        curiosity, community, and love.

* With a nod to Ferlinghetti and William Carlos Williams

Advice from Iowa

Yer burnin daylight, said my mother
as she pulled me up from the sidewalk.
With an old tissue she rubbed the grit
and blood off my greenstick legs.
Many summers ago, she patted me
on the butt, nudged me back outside
into the heat of high summer.

Older now than she was then,
I work through the shortening days,
and the longer nights – writing
pages of lines she will never read.

Notes to the Poems

Pomegranate, a Revision
Rape myths abound in Greek mythology on which so many of our cultural references depend. I contend that to change the culture of the world, we must erase its violent wishful fantasy stories and replace them with tales in which women author their own choices and lives.

Ecology of Fire
May 25, 2018. Ireland votes to repeal the 8th amendment.

Full Circle
The forced migration of people from the land was due to many colliding factors, none laced with kindness. The potato blight repeating over several years coupled with the landowners choice to clear the land for more profitable cattle comes to us through history as The Great Famine. The Gaelic name for that time was *An Gort Mór*, The Great Hunger.

Mea Maxima Culpa
I wrote this after watching the Canadian documentary, Mea Culpa, Mea Maxima Culpa, a report into the clerical abuse of deaf children living at a Catholic institution. Last week I saw a documentary uncovering systemic abuse in England's Protestant Church. Reports roll in from corporations to countries, from Hollywood directors to wrestling coaches, hospitals, and care homes, of abuse from those in power over those who have none. The planet is sick with it. Let's change it.

Mindfulness and Melville
This is a bit of a rant against the designer clad white male gurus who preach solutions to us lesser folk, going for the obvious pun, and having a bit of a laugh at the audacity of such. Meditation is a grand thing, and it is also free.

MEDEA EXPLAINS
Toni Morrison, read in an old newspaper that a slave woman by the name of Margaret Garner was charged with kidnapping and destroying someone else's property. Those few lines became BELOVED, winner of the Pulitzer Prize for fiction in 1987.

THE GYPSY SHAMAN'S DAUGHTER
This timeless goddess – I like to think Denise Kester's cover painting is a likeness of her – was seen to rise from the shores of Fanore, the grey limestone of the Burren and the Cliffs of Moher. From Salthill promenade I watched her stand and take action to catalyse the changes to a better world. I didn't know she was pregnant until I got to the end of the poem. I hope I have done that mother and daughter pair proud.

ENTREPRENEUR FOR MY SEX
Emily Dickinson, Kim Addonizio, Vona Groarke, Adrienne Rich, Maya Angelou, Ntozake Shange, Anna Swir, Zora Neale Hurston are among the many, many women writers so often erased from his story. These and many more celebrate sex as the life force that runs through all of us. A story of domination is rejected for the older story of celebration. 'I can buy my own flowers...' Miley Cyrus. Hoosier's 'Nina Cried Power'.

FELICIA McCARTHY is a poet, writer, scholar and educator. She is a member of Irish PENN. She holds an Honors BA and MA in English Language and Literature from Trinity College, Dublin. She has a second MA in Women's Studies from UCD with a thesis on the poetry of Eavan Boland. She is a creative writing facilitator in both Fingal County Council and Dun Laoghaire-Rathdown County library systems. She lives in Dublin.

Facebook: Felicia McCarthy
Insta: poetry_is_good_medicine
Twitter or X: @falish

Photo: @gerhollandphotography

salmonpoetry

Cliffs of Moher, County Clare, Ireland

"Publishing the finest Irish and international literature."
Michael D. Higgins, President of Ireland